Thomas Edison
TO THE RESCUE!

written by **Howard Goldsmith**

illustrated by **Anna DiVito**

Aladdin

New York London Toronto Sydney Singapore

To Michelle, with love—H. G.
For Gretchen, Annaliese, and Erika Schueler—A. D.

First Aladdin edition January 2003

Text copyright © 2003 by Howard Goldsmith
Illustrations copyright © 2003 by Anna DiVito

ALADDIN PAPERBACKS
An imprint of Simon & Schuster Children's Publishing Division
1230 Avenue of the Americas
New York, NY 10020

Book design by Lisa Vega
The text of this book was set in 18-Point Century Old Style.
The illustrations have been rendered with the Ackerman Pump Pen and watercolor.

Manufactured in the United States of America
4 6 8 10 9 7 5 3

Library of Congress Cataloging-in-Publication Data:

Goldsmith, Howard.
Thomas Edison to the rescue! / by Howard Goldsmith ; illustrated by Anna
DiVito.
p. cm.
Summary: Young Thomas Edison saves a child from being hit by a train
and, as his reward, asks for training as a telegraph operator because
that will help him prepare to become an inventor.
ISBN-13: 978-0-689-85332-6 (ISBN-10: 0-689-85332-7) (library edition)
ISBN-13: 978-0-689-85331-9 (ISBN-10: 0-689-85331-9) (paperback)
1. Edison, Thomas A. (Thomas Alva), 1847–1931—Childhood and
youth—Juvenile literature. 2. Inventors—United
States—Biography—Juvenile literature. 3. Electric engineers—United
States—Biography—Juvenile literature. [1. Edison, Thomas A. (Thomas
Alva), 1847–1931—Childhood and youth. 2. Inventors.] I. DiVito, Anna,
ill. II. Title.
TK140.E3 G65 2003
621.3'092—dc21
2002003382

Young Tom Edison stood
on the Mount Clemens
railroad platform.

"Get your morning newspaper!"
Tom cried.

People rushed past him.

They were running

to catch the train.

"Fresh sandwiches!
Apples, candy!"
Tom shouted.

Tom had made a few dollars
that morning.
"Hey, Tom!" someone called.
Tom turned.

James Mackenzie walked up to him.
Mr. Mackenzie was the
station telegraph operator.

"I will have a ham sandwich,"

Mr. Mackenzie said,

"if you are not too busy."

"Yes, sir," Tom answered,

handing him a sandwich.

Mr. Mackenzie paid Tom.

"Keep the change," he said,

walking away.

"Thank you!" Tom called.

Tom watched a boxcar
roll down the track.
His eyes suddenly
snapped wide open.

Two-and-a-half-year-old
Jimmy Mackenzie
was playing on the track.
"Jimmy, get off the track!"
Tom screamed.
"Hurry! Run!"

Surprised, Jimmy turned
toward Tom's voice.
He froze when he saw the boxcar
rolling straight toward him.
He tried to move,
but he could not.

Tom flew onto the track
and pulled Jimmy away.

A second later
the boxcar roared past.
Tom and Jimmy rolled over
onto the gravel.

"Whew! That was a close call!"

Tom said, breathing hard.

"Are you okay, Jimmy?"

Tom felt Jimmy's arms and legs.

"You look fine," Tom said.

Jimmy's knee was scraped.

But he didn't cry.

His father raced up to them.

"Are you all right, son?"

"He is okay, Mr. Mackenzie," Tom said.

"He is more scared than hurt."

"What happened?"

Mr. Mackenzie asked.

Tom told him about the boxcar.

"Jimmy, I warned you
never to play on the tracks!"
Mr. Mackenzie scolded.
Jimmy broke into tears.

"It's all right, do not cry,"
Mr. Mackenzie said,
hugging his son close.

Mr. Mackenzie turned to Tom.
"How can I ever repay you, Tom?
I am not a rich man, but would
one hundred dollars help?"

"I do not want your money, sir,"
Tom said.
"But could you teach me
to be a telegraph operator?"

"I have read a lot
   about electricity," Tom said.
"I even made my own
   telegraph set."

"I will be happy to teach you, Tom,"

 said Mr. Mackenzie.

"It's the least I can do.

 You are very clever.

 You will learn in no time."

Tom thanked Mr. Mackenzie.

23

Tom lifted Jimmy up.
They walked back
to the station.

"I like to invent things,"
Tom said.
"Learning the telegraph
will help me a lot."

"I am sure electricity
can run lots of things,"
Tom said.

"I suppose so,"
Mr. Mackenzie said,
rubbing his chin.

"Maybe even an electric light!"

Tom exclaimed.

"That would be great!"

"Sure," Mr. Mackenzie said.
"We wouldn't need to use
oil or gas lights.
But do not get ahead of yourself, Tom.
You are just a boy."

"Mom says that every invention began as a dream," Tom answered.

Mr. Mackenzie thought a moment
before answering.

"Your mother is a wise woman, Tom.

I say follow your dream.

You are bound to succeed."

Thomas Edison went on to produce more than one thousand inventions. His inventions changed the world. Many people consider Thomas Edison the greatest inventor of all time.

Here is a timeline of Thomas Edison's life:

1847	Born in Milan, Ohio on February 11
1854	Edison family moves to Port Huron, Michigan
1859	Gets a job selling newspapers and candy on the Grand Trunk Railway
1869	Patents electric vote recorder
1871	Marries Mary Stillwell (Later has three children)
1877	Invents carbon telephone transmitter, improving range and sound of the telephone
1877	Invents the phonograph
1879	Invents long-lasting electric incandescent light bulb
1884	Wife Mary dies
1886	Marries Mina Miller (Later has three more children)
1888	Begins work on the kinetoscope—a motion picture machine (patented in 1894)
1893	Builds first movie studio in West Orange, New Jersey
1908	Invents nickel-iron-alkaline storage battery
1913	Produces talking motion pictures
1928	Awarded Congressional Gold Medal
1931	Dies at home in West Orange at age eighty-four